The DARK STAR GAZER Collection

A. K. Williams

a compilation of poetry, song lyrics and prose

Publishing Coordinator – Sharon Kizziah-Holmes
Cover Photo – NASA Spitzer Space Telescope

Paperback-Press
an imprint of A & S Publishing
A & S Holmes, Inc.

ISBN -13: 978-1-951772-46-8

DEDICATION

This book is dedicated to The Great Divine, to the Angels, to the Sun, the Moon, the Stars, and to the Outsiders.

CONTENTS

ACKNOWLEDGMENTS

I want to thank my husband, X. David Williams, for his encouragement in all my endeavors. I want to thank my children Sophia R. Williams and Olivia D. Williams for inspiring me to want to be better since the days you both were born. I want to thank my mother Leticia Chism, for her angelic care and support, and also my father, Jerry Chism for inspiring me to think farther than my initial thoughts. All mentioned have blessed me a million times and all of them, regardless of everything that might sway them, still believe in me. I love you all. Thank you.

INTRODUCTION

Do you ever feel exhausted? Well, I just want to leave it....
And then once my brain has rested it will be far easier to find the
pathway to the place where all my future poetry sleeps.

Beyond the bridges and the moat,
Past the wall, and the towers, and down the city streets,
Through the orchard, and over the strong current of seven creeks,
Past the prairie of wild flowers that are sipped by golden bees,
To a fertile thriving forest that is ruled by ancient trees,
Where the brush is deep,
And the vines are steep,
And where all the purple spiders sleep,
And there, upon those iridescent webs like dew drops lay,
All the words that each one of my future poems will say.

UNDER THE LOW WANING MOON

T hree lovely souls arrive in the pasture
    Under a low, large, and luminous waning moon
    Mother Moon lays her rays down to capture
The sweet cow and the calf as they groom

One up ahead, dashing quick with the deer
Abreast with the lead and both blazing the way
Their destination ahead is the dark, deep frontier
So one soul slowed and awaited her family of fey

"Here I am, Brother! Here I am, Sister!
A shadow, A shadow, Our shadows away!
God bless this night! So quiet. So bright!
This day was our night and this night is our day!

I'll drink the dark down like a wild, wicked mead!
I'll pray to the God of Good Grace and Good Deeds!
I will rejoice in this time. I will waltz in the weeds!
Our sweet time together again, my brother, my sister, my friends!"

And she looked at her sister, who rode on the wind
Who can be lady, a lily, or lark
Her petals unfurl in the sunbeams
But she'll bloom just as well in the dark

She appeared up high at the crest of the hill
In a glowing silk gown in moonlight
Shimmering like the surface of clear crystal waters
And emitting her own sphere of light

The first of their own Mother's daughters
Born stoic and steady, a spiritual mark
Fundamentally contrasting her frolicking sister
Who could set much on fire with a spark

Then sent to the moon was an arrow
Direct to the orbit from ground
Under dark, starlit skies was their brother
And the hum of bowstring did resound

His frame was as tall as a giant
His broad form an oak in the Forest of Fey
His branches reach up towards the sunbeams
Holding wild choral birds as they pray

Higher and higher he holds them
As they rest in the sunbeams of day
And they pray to the Dear God that molds them
Their songs pierce all the hearts in the grey

Both Lily and Oak look down at their sister
On a hill of wildflowers, a butterfly's park
Like a shadow with mysterious glister

Only few know well enough to remark

The shadow knew that of all the enchanted places
Nothing could quite compare to this pass
She moved and left remnants of true magical traces
As her hands skimmed the top of the grass

Then the shadow, that is she, looked up to starlight
She spoke aloud thoughts that kept her soul fed
And her heart bubbled over with blessings
And not one can forget what she said

"The power of Thee,
The power of Love,
The power of the Great Lord above,
Who lovingly looks upon us three tonight,
And holds each one of us tenderly in this quiet bless-ed moonlight.
How could I ever thank Thee for Thy love,
So pure and true?
How could I ever love you enough?
Your own love as old as a star, as fresh as the dew.
This wondrous life you have given to me,
Forever I am in your debt.
Each day you have been the source of my love,
My Champion!
And I, your devoted pet."

Then... Love, love, love like fuel to the deepest roots from falling
Heaven's rain
A calm, warm wind did sweep the field, and a distant Nightingale
sang
Whatever is to be in life from a Mother's Kiss to Loss's Pain
In that moment the pulse of life was once again revealed
And each heart was a bell that love rang

...

In the Dark, in the Night, in this Field, in the Light
Of the stars, like celestial flowers abloom

They rejoiced for one another, two sisters, one brother
Under a luminous, low waning moon

HAVE YOU EVER HAD
CHAI TEA BEFORE?

I sat down at my table with two tea cups and my father
With my tiny woven bags of tea, and tea pot ready with the water
His hair was salt and peppered, his skin was weathered by the sun
But he's the kind of father, if you are blessed to have, you've won

I kindly placed a tea bag into his little, steamy cup
We began to discuss all kinds of things as we drank the Chai Tea up
From politics, to WWII, to old Egyptian Gods
We mentioned football, and the derby, then we discussed the odds

He took a great big sip, and then I asked him nonchalant
"Have you ever had Chai Tea before", as I passed him a croissant
He coughed, he choked, he coughed again and almost spit it out
I stood to go and help him, I couldn't help but shout

He kindly calmed me with a gesture, and I sat down in my chair
He grinned at me and took a towel that I had lying there
Then he looked out in the distance, through his memories he keenly sorted
And to view the gaze within his eyes, you knew he was transported

And he said...

"Dear daughter," he began, and it was followed with a sigh.

"I drank Chai Tea on the orient with a team of camels trailing by.
Prepared by a young man in a turban, his clothing stitched with jewels and gold.
In a curious Turkish garden where the tea was rich and black and bold.
I gazed across the garden and admired the stunning flora and the fauna.
I watched the sunset on the horizon across the vast Sea of Marmara.

In my ears I heard a skilled man pluck the strings of a wooden oud.
A woman in a golden gown brought me sugared cakes with eastern fruit.
There was a band of brunette beauties, they danced through an emerald gate.
They danced with woven coins that jingled, jangled while I ate.
They danced in many parcels of ginger, cardamom, cinnamon, and cloves.
Some brought in from even farther places, picked up from ships down in the coves.

Then the young man in the turban presented a diamond mortar and its pestle.
He ground up all the spices within that ornate ancient vessel.
Upon the center of a silver tray was a tea cup made of pearl.
And he poured the Chai Tea in and I watched it's creamy, frothy swirl.
I stirred it with an opal spoon made by monks in old Beijing.
And if for only just one moment…... I thought I was a king.

So... yes I have drank Chai before, in a foreign charming land.
And I would encourage all to drink it, and drink a lot of it if you can.
But this tea is exquisite, and my daughters are all exquisite too.
And what makes this Chai Tea the very best is that I'm drinking it with you."

Then he looked at me from across the table with a twinkle in his
eye
And his words held so much beauty that I thought that I would cry
His hair was salt and peppered, his skin was weathered by the sun
But he's the kind of father, if you are blessed to have, you've won

BOXCAR BEATRIX AND THE
TIME MACHINE

(Song Lyrics)

Boxcar Beatrix, your dress is a mess, girl
You're the prettiest girl that I've seen
We stopped by the fountain on the way to our adventure
And quickly we filled our canteens
Then we took a train to the moon one day
And we planted a handful of beans
Then we climbed up a vine to our castle and read magazines

Boxcar Beatrix, you are my confidant
And I am your best friend it seems

We boarded our boat by the pier in the forest
And mapped all the brooks and the streams
Then boldly we fired our cannons
And we saved all the priests and the queens
Then we stepped into pink gowns and jumped into white
limousines

Boxcar Beatrix, you are my best girl
And I am the friend of your dreams
We sat by the fire, we sang like a choir
We laughed till we burst at the seams
And I would not ever betray you
And you would never betray me
And we swore on the stars that I'd always have you and you'd
have me

Boxcar Beatrix, you're more than just a girl
You are my best friend it seems
We stood on a map, you chose East ,I chose West
That's the last time we were ever seen
And I cannot ever replace you
And, no, you cannot replace me
But I'm drawing up blueprints and building a new time machine

ABUELO'S AVOCADO TREE

By a sturdy house in Mayaguez grows an Avocado Tree
It is tended by the sun and rain and grows abundantly
The fruit it bears is heavy with its marrow greenish yellow
Its trunk is steep, its roots are deep, and it belongs to Dear Abuelo

Abuelo looks up from the trunk, surveys its yield both tall and
wide
The fruit is heavy and branches sunk, let all be blessed, let Earth
provide
He takes his ladder, climbs it high, both sight and touch will be his
guide
Then still a week before it's eaten when the meat is soft inside

As patient as the sun, as patient as the moon
As patient as the wind, the seas, and as constant as the island
bloom
For years, when it was young, the tree only provided shade
But Abuelo knew the day would come, and he would reap the
fruits it made

Then the winds blew heavy, and stripped it down to skin below the
bark
No leaves, no branches, no avocados, just a stump left in the dark
Abuelo stood and shook his head, his faithful friend had lost it all
But in the rain and whipping winds, it did not fall, it did not fall

He began to nurse the tree, with extra food and care
And it grew stronger every day because it knew that he was there
Till once again it bore its fruits, a yield both tall and wide
From tallest leaves to deepest roots, let all be blessed, let Earth
provide

There's a sturdy house in Mayaguez with an Avocado Tree
It is tended by the sun and rain and grows abundantly
The fruit it bears is heavy with its marrow greenish yellow
Its trunk is steep, its roots are deep, and it belongs to Dear Abuelo

THE CROW SOUL SISTERS

All three crow sisters sat down for some tea, at an octagon table by the pink plumes of a tree.

All their shiny black feathers, which they ruffled, then sat, on an iron garden chair, with their smartly cocked hat.

And lying flat 'round their necks was a fine string of pearls, formed in mollusks in meadows under pond water swirls.

They were comfortable as such, no buzz, and no quandary, as they sat and sipped tea and they aired dirty laundry;

About the pigs, and the dogs, and all the jackasses, all kinds, from each level, from all social classes.

Their unparalleled sass, as words rolled off their tongue, the speeches they crowed, the declarations they sung.

From the mild sideways snip, to a roaring Hell Fire, either one crow's revelation, or all join in like a choir.

Each did have their tea cup, one, two, and three, one for each sister, obviously.

How dainty the creamer and broad sugar bowl, and a fourth tea cup set out to make lighter the soul.

Long ago they'd decided about that fourth cup of tea, as they aired out their grievances confidently.

That cup is for worries, that cup is for fears, a representation of frustration and tears.

When each said out loud what bound their heart up, they'd drop one cube of sugar right into that cup.

And all the truths at the table are locked tight in three beaks. In a murder of crows, what they say is for keeps.

They lay out their grievance, their spirits less weighted, till the world lifts from their shoulders, and their anger's sedated.

What a beautiful thing, all their worries besieged, as they reach in their hearts and they rip out the weeds.

From three eggs they were hatched, and when that nest was their bed, they remembered a time when their wise mother said,

"Despair is the enemy of all hopes and all dreams. It will crush all your spirits and clip all your wings.

Cast it out rightly! Stomp it under your claw!" Then she soared out of sight with a loud regal CAW!

They mention her words while they straightened their hats, and they uncoiled their pearls, and they tidied placemats.

Now that fourth cup is full and too sweet to the taste, 'cause their words flowed like rivers when their outrage was faced.

But before they depart, they do something profound, they tip the fourth cup of tea and pour it over the ground.

As it soaks into the Earth they all stomp it away, and their spirits are lighter, and brighter their day.

Dear Indigo and Sweet Clementine

Phantom floating helix of spinning copper leaves
Let dusk ignite all Jack-o-Lantern shrines!
Oh, great enchanted night, under shadows and silver light
Danced our Dearest Indigo and our Sweet, Sweet Clementine

"How do you do, Sweet Sugar Moon?
Could take all night to recite the tally of your charms."
Then both dip low a curtsy for the eventide
Then rise, swinging wild and spinning in each other's arms

Cherub cheeked, Sweet Clementine, feline in witches hat
Dear Indigo, red horned, with lovely mask of sapphire jewels
Both have longed to rule the kingdom of this night, shining bright!
Rise! The majesty of children within this theater of grown fools

Painted tree branch for enchanted, pearly scepter
A tall crown of royal, silver heather, weaved
Collecting loot from every wolf and wispy specter
Fun follies and a sugar feast, both ardently received

Behold the evenings promenade, one mile long and serpentine
Rolling wagons full of pumpkins, who cast a toothless, orangey
glow
Imagination engines fueled by the bless-ed blue moonbeams
Encouraged minds build fountains where sound aspirations flow

I spy with my cyclops eye two lovely Halloween Queens
From all blooming, budding children do the wisest spirits grow
Raise up high your scepters, manifest your hopes and dreams
It begins first within the mind and then you'll watch your kingdom
grow

PETRIFIED CRUMBS

(must be recited with disgust)

Oh, the horror I see!
Repulsive, Petrified Crumbs!
When I flipped my old couch on its side
I found socks that were stinky
And an old ancient Twinkie
And some twisties my cat tried to hide

Oh, the horror I see!
Repulsive, Petrified crumbs!
I cannot fathom what you must have been
The crumbs of pork pie, and the wings of some fly
Who'd succumbed to an unfortunate end

Run and fetch me my broom!
Quick the bleach and the mop!
I must be rid of this strange mix of waste!
This vile potpourri in a pile before me
Must be removed with spectacular haste!

Oh, the horror, the horror of petrified crumbs!
Minuscule splinters and dander of beasts!
Remnants of candy as old as your granny!
A bug corpse from an old spider's feast!

Off, off, into the bin!

I will think of your foulness no more!
This broom and this dust pan both mean I will win!
To the trash!
Through the room!
Out the door!

THE RED PARASOL AND THE ROOSTER, DREAD

I stepped out of my car at my parent's home after work and I heard their rooster crow from the large chicken yard. It's a heartwarming sound to hear a rooster crow, but if you know this particular rooster the first feeling you have when you hear his distant crow is gratefulness. Grateful that he's over there and you're over here. The rooster at my parent's house hates everyone. He does not acknowledge friendship or acquaintances from people that pass in and out of the yard. What he acknowledges is his territory and his harem of hens, and if you enter his territory it's an affront to him which he immediately addresses. So, when I meander across the field to see the cow or visit the hens I am always mindful of him because I may have to defend myself. Even my mother doesn't go near without a stick or something to swing in case of a dreaded confrontation. Since this story mentions more than one rooster, I will refer to this large, mean one as Dread. The name happens to suit the ambiance of his presence.

Today right after the rooster crowed I heard another crow from a different rooster. I could tell by the sound of it that it was from one much smaller than Dread. There were several Leghorn chickens purchased many weeks ago. They were kept separate while they were small and introduced into the main flock once large enough to handle themselves amongst the older chickens. Older chickens can be quite cruel to a new younger flock or any new inductees in general. The pecking order is real and chickens don't mess around. You are either above them or below them and they will treat you accordingly. Currently, the new flock of Leghorns are running with the old flock of Buff Orpingtons, Rhode Island Reds, etc. Two of those new chickens happen to be roosters.

I thought the crow from the young rooster was adorable and decided that I had to see this new upcoming Leghorn. I began to search for a weapon to protect myself. In my defense I have never struck Dread. He is quick and will instinctively protect his hens, which is what he is designed to do ...with the sharp spurs on his legs, and in all honesty I can dislike this bird but I can't hate him. He does a good job. But since I didn't want to be assaulted, I grabbed my red parasol which happened to be in the trunk of the car.

I wasn't sure if it would really help me. I had never tried this before and previously had picked up sticks or a nearby rake to swing at Dread when he charged at me. But he never feared me or anything in my hands. I would swing wide and he would just step back uncaring of my defense, all the while eyeing for an opening to launch his attack (opportunistic jerk). Sometimes I would pound the ground with a stick and shout like a crazy person but this rooster was not scared of crazy. He might backup and give you the sense that he's going to leave you alone, but don't turn around. He likes to charge when you do.

I walked around the side of the house to the chicken yard where the foliage and trees are thriving and the grass is only this certain shade of deep green in the Spring. The bugs are plentiful, and all chicken bellies are full. Peaceful, a spacious place, a chicken paradise, and they were all out foraging in the fresh grass and thickets, all except Dread who was on the lookout for trespassers. He sees me at the gate and I see him. My red parasol down at my side like a sword. I opened the gate. The trespasser.

I could see in his eyes that he wanted to cause me great harm, and in his chicken daydreams was probably dancing around my dead corpse, but I was determined to see the Leghorn and I would not be deterred by fear. I took a step in. He took a step toward me. It was a duel. He and his spurs and myself with my red parasol. I extended it out toward him and peered down its length. He took another step toward me. I placed my finger carefully on the button of my device, which is customary for most umbrellas/parasols, the automatic open button. And then I pushed it. Whoosh!

Oh, the terror! The wings flailing about. Tiny chicken legs running for dear life. Scattering to the farthest edges of their paradise which was now inhabited by a beast with a red parasol. They hid behind the farthest tree trunks and bushes.

There stood Dread with an obvious internal struggle. He was just as terrified. He'd never seen a weapon such as this. He had receded some but had not scattered to the edges like the others. First of all, he was the boss of this place, and secondly, the hens were watching. I closed my parasol but kept my eyes on him. Your move, I thought. I had a confidence he had never witnessed before. That confidence paired with my perceived deadly weapon made him very unsure. And, oh, the look in his eyes! Pure hatred. But I could tell he was slowly recovering, so once again I raised my parasol and pressed the button. Whoosh! Then he began to run and I chased him. For once it was me chasing him! And I laughed like an idiot and raised my hands up to the sky in the center of that chicken paradise and shouted "Victory!"

I walked over to the bushes and trees where the other chickens were hiding and knelt down to have a look at the Leghorns. I tried to coax them out by talking sweetly to them, my back to Dread who I noticed was across the field. I had won the battle and he would not tangle with the lady with the parasol any more today. Then I saw the rooster, a young snow white Leghorn with a bright red comb. Another one of God's creations, perfect in every way. I secretly hoped one day we'd be friends although that's not likely. Not impossible, but not likely.

I decided to get going and I moved across that yard with a swagger I may never be able to replicate outside of that situation. I took my time. My parasol rested on my shoulder and my head was high. I was completely unafraid, and I would not be chased out of the yard today. Dread stood behind some weeds and peered at me. Clucking angrily. And I pointed my parasol at him as I walked through the gate.

OH, BLACK COFFEE!

Oh, black coffee!
Black, black dew
So strong that I can almost chew
Dark elixir of exotic beans
The fuel of champions, the oomph of queens
When my peepers spy the morning sun
I raise my covers to hide my face
But obligations I can't outrun, and this day's a gift I can't replace
Shake awake my spirit, open wide my eyes
And help my sleepy body rise, rise, rise!
Drifting to the coffee pot, like a drooling un-dead hag
I stumble through my quiet house
Step, drag, step, drag, step, drag
But each sip relights my consciousness
I bloom each dawn by the blending of our chemistry
Until the singing of the morning birds begins to sound like
heartfelt ministry
I know that I rely on you too much, on your daily morning magic I
do ardently depend
Oh, dear coffee if you were a human being, you would be my
dearest friend

HIPS

My hips are like hills that extend from my spine
They are not small hips, they are large, they are mine
And I've finally decided that they are just fine
I was built to bear children, during childbearing time

I was designed to have babies on a mountain alone
And SURVIVE! Then arrive! With a child of my own!
By the sweat of my brow, when each pang rang a bell
My soul was exposed and I pushed from its well

Then a healthy new life, in the image of the Divine
From the center of Heaven, was plucked from the vine
Then down through two hips that are round, that are wide
The way of my hips allowed us to survive

The curve, the width, the weight on the bone
I was designed to have babies on a mountain alone
They are primitive, a gift that my Maker did give
My hips were designed so that I could live

THROW MARIGOLD SEEDS UPON MY GRAVE

When old queens depart, and their babies raised
Throw marigold seeds upon my grave
When a coward evolves to be bold and brave
Throw marigold seeds upon my grave
When daisy chains sit on crowns of true loves gaze
Throw marigold seeds upon my grave
When a truth is said, and to the hearts it saves
Throw marigold seeds upon my grave

Just throw them 'cause I'll be long dead
And their tiny roots will grow

A. K. WILLIAMS

Into the ground, into my head
Then my sleeping soul will know
That not forgotten is a dreamer's hope
They'll be no dusty pages lost to dark
As two poets let our hearts elope
And let no time tear us apart

BE LIGHT

(Song Lyrics)

We must go on till the fire is done
Even with small embers at night
Sorry souled, sad, and feeling glum
When the shadows shift into your light

The sweet sun will crest on yonder hill
And the brooks whisper sonnets at night
But isn't our armor heavy still
Long days lead to battles we fight

So let's cross the pass by the old wooden house
Where we skimmed stones on still waters
We'll go to the place beyond the hill
We'll hold tight our sons and our daughters

Even old stars do burn away
Oh, the moon counts each night by its face
So, bow your head mother it's time to pray
For love, divine courage, and grace

When it's all done and the fire is gone
And the brooks whisper sonnets at night
All but our soul, the Earth swallows us whole
So let our hearts and our spirits be light

THE CANTANKEROUS FATHER OF THE BRIDE

There was a hush in the room when the bride's father spoke
Enough you could hear a mouse whisper
The sweat on the brow of both bride and the groom
Now passed to all kin from Great Grandma to sister

The cantankerous father, but quite right in the mind
Committed for life to protect all that he loved
His family his treasure, his opinions refined
So, all his words spoken are all spoken un-gloved

The blunder was due to the Magistrate
He spoke, "Who gives this daughter away?"
The response from the dear brides old father
Not one will forget for the rest of their days....

"No, I won't say it!
Absolutely not!
You must make a change to that long held tradition.
I won't give my daughter away, I will not!
Not under any condition!
I know this is her wedding.
I know this is her day.
You may kindly just ask my permission.
But to agree to give my own lovely daughter away!?
You misunderstand my position!
I did not have my children to give them away,

Though, I will permit her to wed this young chap.
But if he ever does harm to my dear, lovely daughter
I will hunt him and give him the strap!
I will not interfere in their union.
They are bound to argue, their own ups and their downs.
That is the nature of marriage,
Independent minds may have verbal rounds.
I will expect that they both cherish each other.
I expect that they uphold their vows.
But if I see my daughter with an abused, broken spirit
I will happily feed him to sows! (gasp from the crowd)
My daughter's all grown, and my heart's a bit broken,
By night I'll be drunken with mead.
But now that we all understand one another,
Magistrate! You may proceed!"

DEAR YOUNG PUMPKIN FELLOW

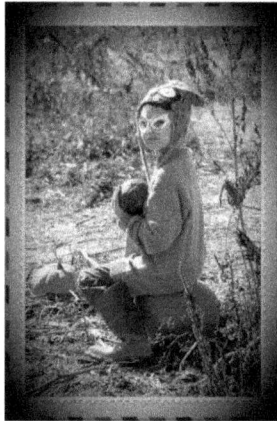

Dear Young Pumpkin Fellow
Running through the pumpkin field
With your arms around round pumpkins
Amongst the full fresh harvest yield

So proud you are of this charge
Wide smile on ruddy cheeks
It's as if you've been here all along
And have been doing this for weeks

Eyes of joy and an Autumn soul
Is what I see today
A foot alight in open fields
And Winter at its bay

Pumpkin picker frolicking
'Round vines and nature's sprout
It's as if you know there's something more
Something others live without

And then I looked and began to believe…

And then I felt and began to believe…

And then I believed….

There is a danger to have no pumpkin
In the throes of chilly Fall
'Cause if you have no pumpkin
You may not be synced with Fall at all

You may see the falling leaves
You may feel the chilly winds
But with no pumpkin to call your own
You've missed Autumn's dearest kin

So I said I had no pumpkin
And he ran with all his might
To retrieve a plump, round pumpkin
Before the carriage took its flight

He took his time in picking
Plucked from vine so carefully
And my heart then nearly burst with joy
When he delivered it to me

Oh, what a beautiful pumpkin!
Glorious! Fall! Divine!
You've grown for me most patiently
Till plucked from your own vine

Then I looked unto my sister
And saw two arms unfilled
And I shouted, "Dear Young Pumpkin Fellow,

My sister's heart's un-thrilled!

Please fetch a pumpkin right away
And she'll enjoy this season.
'Twill fill her heart with happiness
There can be no better reason.

For every year we'll have a pumpkin
For just as long as we can breathe,
Because sometimes simple happiness
Is easily achieved."

She said, "I dare say you're ridiculous!
I need no pumpkin to make my soul anew!"
But when he placed it on her lap
There was not one smile but two

So, don't forget your pumpkin
Not for any reason
Pick a pumpkin at the very least
To celebrate the season

I shan't forget that Autumn day
Our spirits content and mellow
Nor the smile and ruddy cheeks of that
Sweet and Dear Young Pumpkin Fellow

THE BOG OF THE BARONESS

Many, many moons ago in a town near bustling Budapest
Lived two lovers, whose love through centuries known,
the Baron and the Baroness

On the 13th moon that filled the night, full round edge and glowing true
Twas like a cyclops in the night whose eye rested on the sainted two

And saw beneath its starry brethren, all abloom, the gentle bow of Cupid's lips
But love doth fall as lovers go like elemental comet trips

A blessed wedding. Oh! wondrous day. The lovers moved as true love goes

A night, a month, and then a day, then the parting of the lovely pair arose

A voyage set heretofore, before gentle stroke of Venus fold
But naught would blur their beating hearts cause both were pure and both were bold

But the Baron's ship on port did call, he bid farewell amongst wooden mast
And that night the blue sea stole it all, and their parting kiss would be their last

Many, many moons the Baroness lay with silver tears on velvet cheeks
She waited for the Baron's ship, she waited for a thousand weeks

All about knew the echoes of her cries, as she bid Poseidon set her beloved free
'Cause she feared on the bottom earth he lay, under leagues, under sea

Her father moved her far away to inland moors, one moonlit night
Away from salty air and crashing tides, to landlocked peace and life's new light

But even though she had no sea, to cast her weary gaze
She graced the frame of window sill for a hundred thousand days

Years came of torrential rain, and what was moor became a bog
The moor grew even darker still and glowed an eerie purple fog

Where bullfrogs slept and the viper dreamt, a land of marshy grass
Where melodic dancing purple gases might let any specter pass

And on an eve through the foggy mist, she saw an eerie purple mast
And on the bow the ghostly Baron stood, she saw his ship at last

Floating in the cold night air, the spectral vessel lit with a majestic

violet light
She joined the Baron on the ship and was never seen after that
night

Now it's been two hundred years, and the purple bog lights never
rest
They dance because of Love's most true, the Baron and the
Baroness

MR. VESPER SASSAFRAS

(the truth teller)

Mister Vesper Sassafras
You sit so wise with words astute
Beady, root beer colored eyes
Paired with olive green, expensive suit

Refined so in your style and poise
Not one can match your sharpened mind
And most who've tried have went kaput
Their egos likened to a bird's behind

One perception is one angle
With one angle, by God, he's bored
His joy in life is undoing tangles
When there's many chips upon the board

When he lifts his cerebral blade of Samurai
And holds it to his opponent's blade of grass
It moves through it without resistance
Both splitting atoms, splitting mass

When his opponent pales within defeat
Caused by authentic words that cast a blow
He remains unmoved within his seat
Watching his rival's composure bow

But Mister Vesper Sassafras
Does not care to win or lose
His mind is bored in telling lies
His mind is set on telling truths

A broader mind is something new
From said opponent, if ego would allow
But to be defeated in wit and view
Is a disheartening field to plow

Let the wisest take the pain
And the beating of their ego bruised
From an honest man, well read, un-reigned
Is a good man should your battle lose

THE GHASTLY GOBLIN GARDEN

There's a Ghastly Goblin Garden in every well-established town
And all of these ghastly gardens are never destined to be found
But...To find one first find the trunk of a long dead willow tree
Go 'round seven times clockwise, then go 'round backwards three

Then you'll see a new dimension, a beguiling, bewitching place
And there! Do you see the rusty gate adorned with spider's lace?
Beyond it spans a stately garden where deathly plants do grow
It's a garden, but a monstrous place, it's where the goblins go

When they tire of doing mischief, and they yawn and rub their eyes
And the light does tax their bodies, and they curse the new blue skies

They march themselves around that tree, then through the gate to shadows deep
Then all the goblins go to bed, like wolf pups in a giant heap

Now your bravery has got you this far, so begin to move your feet
But beware of everything that grows, even docile looking peat
And there are insects here of a most devastating kind
Some can cut you ear to ear, and some can make you blind

Tie a blessed red string to the gate so you don't lose your way
This garden is not only full of goblins but it's also full of fey
An iron bell you should find near the gloomy entrance way
Pick it up you fool! You'll have to ring it or the fairies might make you stay!

Beware of the vines of the Snagglefoot, and the Bloodwick of East Viper Bay
The latter a blood drinking flower, drinks it up like a fine Cabernet
A poisonous paralytic by the scent or the touch, then you quickly become flower prey
The former has immeasurable power and will choke you then drag you away

Mind your footing near the black water pool, no one knows its depth
And there's a nest of flattened grass where something large has slept
It may be in the water, where the vicious, blue piranha feeds
Don't get too close! It's watching! There are red eyes in the reeds!

Just keep walking down the path, don't drag your feet or whistle
Go past the Raven's silver bath and Deadly Witches Thistle
Observe the flourishing Tempest Dahlias, their roots lay underfoot
Deep down to molten lava, one sniff you turn to soot

If something taps your shoulder it may be the Fiendish Trees
They will wrap you in their branches and feed you to their leaves
Mind the Murder Maple and its tricky, trapping sap
It will drag you to its teethy trunk and Snap! Snap! Snap!

Then the path splits 'round a fountain, at center stands a crystal
fairy queen
But things born of that realm are never as innocent as they seem
By a bench around the fountain where the Golden Ivy creeps
Expect to see a little child, and in her hands she weeps

Bring the bell up at the ready, don't be convinced to stay
You will feel compelled to help her, it appears she's lost her way
But I bid you, keep on walking she's from the Dana O'Shee
That would be another journey, and we don't have time today

The bell is to dispel glamour so ring it if you must
But when you do it seems to cause an awful kind of fuss
The things born of the fairy realm do not like to be found out
And we are here to see the goblins, to get in, and then get out

Now look down at your feet, the gentle turning path of dark mosaic
stones
There is an insect on the trail ahead that will bite you and turn you
to bones
It looks like a newly plucked daisy, inviting, and fragrant, and true
But it's venom is potent and violently deadly, so don't let this
happen to you

Just up ahead around the bend, you will see where the goblins
sleep
Pass by the old haunted graves, their headstones tilted like old
jagged teeth
And many pale ghosts will grab you, drag you down flailing to a
fiery sea
Unless you cross your heart five times, then they have to set you
free

Now! Do you see a dense and dreadful fog? Do you hear the Hell
Hounds bay?
Right below that Harpy Tree is where the goblins lay!
In between two mausoleums where the gargoyles gulp the rain
Lies a giant pile of devil beasts who are vile and quite insane

Some no bigger than a foot, some are four foot, some are two
There just might be a hundred, of this repulsive, rotten crew
Their noses are all piggish, and their green skin slimy slick
And they've never known a bar of soap, so, Boy! That stench is thick!

Tiptoe round them if you must, don't make a lot of noise
Mind the ancient urns and flower vases, you don't wish to wake these kind of boys
You have made it! You have seen them! Your courageous quest is done!
Watch it! Watch it! Watch it! Crash! Now look what you have done!

Oh no! They all are waking, and they have seen that you are here!
In my own soul I am shaking with the deepest kind of fear!
You have no other choice, they are rising one-by-one
I'm afraid your only option is TO RUN! RUN! RUN!

Note ***Written to be read aloud but must be practiced first, of course. I would encourage all to snap their hands together in an alligator-type fashion when you get to the portion of the poem that reads, Snap! Snap! Snap! (the end of the 9th stanza, dead center), and this is because the poem is a little lengthy, and a large alligator-type clapping of the hands should snap any child out of any slight lethargy they may be experiencing due to its length (surely, not its content). I must express my pride in its length because it is 18 stanzas just like my favorite poem The Raven by Poe (although his stanzas are 6 lines each and mine are only 4). Howbeit, read it to your favorite children, either goblins or humans will do. The end reaction will depend on the crowd. The goblins will probably cheer. The humans will probably shriek.

THE PURGATORY TRAIN OF THE PROPER

Within the hearts of each one of us are pulses of living electrical energy that carry us until death. The very first time our heart beats is when it begins. How it gets there is another story but according to some at the time of our "departure" that energy dissipates into the atmosphere, transposing itself from electrical to thermal, never to be seen or heard from again in this dimension, or in this lifetime. Another theory all together is that it can draw itself in at will and create a manifestation, a wispy reproduction of its former self.

There are many of those wispy reproductions that regularly stroll down Main Street in town. Down our mortal street, moving either West or East; stepping with their translucent tipping bowler hats and erected parasols, vests and starched evening jackets, and rustling skirts with petticoats. Some flaunt bold white powdered wigs. Others hold wands with jeweled masks on their ends that are held up to cold and weightless, airy faces. And through those masks should stare out two phantom eyes, but in their cases there are none. Each and every one utterly eye-less. Their dark, deep, and abysmal eye sockets are positively chilling to stare into. Nonetheless the wraiths never miss a step and address all their fellows and maidens by name. They do not fidget about but line the concrete walks and strive forward with purpose and destination. They really are such a lovely and ghastly group. A mass of parading shadows in the white moonlight.

This group of specters congregate every evening in the vicinity of the current weekly farmers market near the railroad tracks in The Proper. The Proper is the oldest part of the town where all the buildings tower near the railroad tracks, the primary lifeline of the town's industry in days past. Those steel tracks have run through The Proper for over a hundred years. They were laid over wooden rail ties cut by backwoods brawny lumberjacks, sold for five cents each and affixed to the ground with carbon steel spikes; the heads of such driven in by the throw of large sledge hammers by impressively powerful men. If you stand at the tracks and turn your head from left to right they appear to be infinite as they either bend out of sight or continue on straight but surpass the limits of your beyond yonder vision. A symbol of industry and growth in the days of horse and carriage. Whether once fueled by steam or the current diesel, whether passenger or cargo, the rumbling of those grand metal machines has resonated through the town, rattling plates in cupboards and waking babies from their sound sleeps for a century.

A forgotten depot partially stands near the tracks, grown up with honeysuckle, half collapsed in the shadows of weeds. The trunk of an oak triumphantly bursting through its rotten floor boards, green leaves bending in the breeze this way and that, waving to both the sun and the moon. Here. This is exactly where the phantoms meet. They converse excitedly with each other about many things, refreshed each night, reborn, reformed, and reunited in the heart of The Proper with an almost family like pride, because regardless of their origin, night after night, they suffer the same fate together.

There was a circle of spirits around the stately ghost, Jim Meredith, who was discussing the night Lincoln was assassinated. He was just a living boy at his mother's knee when he heard the dreadful news and had a cousin who was at the theater on the night of the president's murder. This cousin had divulged the details of the sorrowful event which Jim had relayed numerous times in his life, just as he was doing this night. "Poor soul," someone said. "Poor soul you say?" Said Jim. "Well, I say that Lincoln never was, never has been, and never will be a poor soul. Never is a poor soul one that the Lord keeps. I don't doubt for one moment that Lincoln was delivered by the Angels straight to the doors of Heaven. Look around you! We are the poor souls!" A sound declaration, and everyone in earshot quieted somberly for a moment in agreement until someone randomly shouted, "Would someone please pour my poor soul a drink then!" Laughter erupted under the dark sky as their joy was re-found and the conversations continued. Even Jim shook his head and chuckled deeply. Long ago they had accepted their purgatory fates but it still was not a beloved topic of conversation, and though they may have been granted a stint in purgatory they were not denied their joy or sense of humor. When a whistle blew in the distance all conversations dwindled down to near nothing and all apparitions anticipated the approach of their nightly train.

Each night when the church bell chimes twelve, the tolling is trailed by the blow of a whistle from a ghostly pale steam engine. A serpentine locomotive pulling passenger cars and pounding its pistons, crankshafts, and connecting rods. Rolling and rumbling phantom wheels under bizarre and finely chiseled cars adorned with chubby grinning cherubs and perched goblins. Upon the engine rests a giant open mouthed serpent head with two long translucent fangs, and two nostrils exhausting steam, and in the eye sockets of the snake's head are two diamond human skulls reflecting the silver moonlight. Then at the rear of the caboose is a throne where a chiseled reaper sits, his scythe extended towards the Heavens like an un-waving flag.

This steam fueled passenger train was once a wondrous sight in our own dimension, but its physical self currently lies in a train yard five hundred miles away. An abandoned and forgotten remnant of its former self. Even so, its splendor could not be put to bed when the rust had nearly eaten it whole. The walls of each car bore witness, in their own sense, to all spectrums of human energies from the emission of new love to violent robbery, and maintained, after its own form of death, within each iron bolt of its structure, a whisper of all that once was. That whisper sparked the creation of what is now a grandiose supernatural engine far finer than what had existed before. If only you could see the phantom train with your own eyes you would be in awe of its wildly intricate and byzantine beauty.

When it comes to a complete stop in front of the phantoms the engine makes a sound like the sighing of a giant dragon. The crowd aglow in a moon silver shade wait as seven crew members descend. They are immortal beings that were never human at all. Tall, narrow and spindly; resembling the human form and yet something most definitely askew about it, but all finely dressed in jackets and bow ties, cuff links and boots. A novel sight they are with the most interesting bright eyes a little larger than they should be with lids that blink lazily over slit pupils. They assist the ladies in their boarding and dip their heads low to the men. They are the most cordial and attentive servants. Each one with a name tag over their right breast and each plate reads as follows: Gluttony, Wrath, Envy, Pride, Lust, Greed and Sloth. These are the crewmen of the train.

The conductor's name is Isaac. He is a towering man, burly and broad. His eyes are radiant with a silver glowing light. He is clearly not from the same dimension as we and the current smoky concentration of his being is not a mere shadow of his former self but is in fact his eternal form. He wears a long jacket and a full white braided beard that extends down to the middle of his chest. He not only has the duty of the train itself, a stewardship given to him by an even greater supernatural being from an unknown origin, but he also keeps the purgatory time of the guests. He winds his silver pocket watch and dons his conductors hat before stepping from the car and sweeping through the ghostly assembly. He weaves in and out of the congregation tapping ghosts on their shoulders, calling them by their name and declaring, "Your time is served." At once those specters vanish into the dark night never again to witness the grandiose train before them. Once he has completed his initial duties. He steps up into the entryway of the engine and shouts, "All Aboard!!"

When the first otherworldly foot of the assembly touches the steps each vaporous spirit begins a nightly decay until death. All had met their true death long ago, but even so they are forced to meet it again every night. The course is slow and starts with their attire going from pristine to threadbare, but there are many trains to be visited and the phantoms are not accustomed to letting a little death and decay get in the way of their merriment. Indeed most of the ghosts are now feeling particularly famished, a tax from their earlier stroll, and begin their evening with a royal dinner in the dining cars.

Gluttony keeps the dining cars going with roasted pigs, potatoes, and succotash. Thick gravies roll over biscuits and briskets. The finest cuts of meat are rubbed in the rarest, most delicious and most fragrant of spices. There are sweet smelling fruit pies and towering cakes. The specters gather around the luxurious banquet as they take their seats in high backed chairs around long bejeweled tables. The wine flows abundantly from crystal glasses to smoky lips. Candelabras are set at intervals between the dinner guests each burning, flickering blue flames. The divine dishes are passed around, the rolls, the butter, the potatoes and the gravy boats, but not one soul fills their plate in a mountainous pile. All are mindful that their evening is only beginning. Gluttony, by dinner's end, always feels a slight sense of panic but hides it well behind a jolly slant of a smile. No one is stupid with wine to his great dismay, and before they are overly full, they leave.

Now everyone knows that Sloth is a terrible bore. It is true that one might attempt to sleep their time in purgatory away, burdened in misery, but why would one want to? Most tire rather quickly of being so still and desolate. "Woe is me. I was turned away at Heaven's gate!" Some sob similar remarks while Sloth does his rounds and tucks all the spirits in, "There, there, my child." There is no lack of comfort here. There is no poor service. The cars that Sloth circulates provide the highest amenities; down coverings and down pillows over satin sheets of the utmost superior quality. Tightly drawn drapes so the sleeping passengers won't be disturbed by seeing the landscape of the world around them passing by. He would much prefer that you come after overeating or after having too much to drink and have come to sleep it off; but he'll take what he can get and you won't have to atone or absolve a thing. You can lay there until your bones begin to turn partially to dust, but not to worry, Sloth will shake the sheets out for you and make sure that your bones are returned to their rightful place before dawn and the train will be there from tomorrow's midnight until eternity.

The challenge for each spirit in a sleeping car is that they have the knowledge that the next car over is filled with delightful music and dancing, and that knowledge alone will fester in a phantom's head creating the feeling that they are missing out on something wonderful. That is always enough to keep one from sleeping, and is equivalent to being poked in the head by a stray pillow quill unmercifully. Soon enough the sleeper chooses to rise from their bed. They kick off their coverings, smooth out their clothes, and move to the next car to partake in the wonders of the train that are promptly available to them.

Nonetheless, after dinner the spirits are even more "worse for wear." And those who chose not to attempt to sleep their time away make their way to the lounging cars to play games and enjoy music. Their fresh translucent but lustrous complexions from earlier have developed a sickly pallor and gauntness. They grip their poker cards with more bone than flesh. The men puff their cigars sparingly and study their cards concentrating on their next move.

Greed runs the Pharaoh table but is a terrible cheat and everyone has learned long ago never to play with him. All the guests have permanently banned him from the poker tables. He is a sweet talker, very convincing in his suggested strategies, and focused but cannot be trusted. Greed, in conversation, is very good at convincing others that their personal value is reflected in their pile of chips, and cheating others in order to win is always a part of his recommendations. If anybody would only listen to him! Oh, how he relishes watching a phantom take the last chip from a fellow passenger. But here on the train all apparitions see greed plainly and his encouragement falls on deaf ears. Most annoyingly all the winnings at the game's end are returned to the original owner and the gamblers enjoy the game for the sport of it, not for what they can accumulate and take away from one another. Greed spends the latter of the morning bored and sulking and becomes a wicked grouch. This doesn't win him any friends, but everyone knows that he was never looking for friends. It's not in his design.

Envy is always whispering in someone's ear and it's usually about how somebody else has won. Josephine, a ghost that is half a century old plays Bridge at one of the card tables. She wears a dress belted at the waist with five pearl buttons up the front. She wears white gloves with lace at the cuffs, and her silver hair is twisted up and smoothed back into a clip. She smiles generously and brightly at her fellow players. Their living family is the current topic of discussion, which is the most joyous discussion for ones of their kind. A beloved great, great, granddaughter has gone to the Pacific for a stay at Josephine's old beach house and has found a long-lost pair of earrings. The earrings were sent to Josephine from

Egypt by a dear lover. A lover who had died in an accident when Josephine was twenty five. She did grow to love other men but none as much as she loved him. Those earrings were the last gift he gave to her. They were removed before bed one night and never again found in her lifetime.

On her deathbed she mentioned to her daughter that she wished she knew where they were. She would have loved to have been buried with those earrings, an homage to the afterlife of the Kings and Queens of ancient Egypt, but mostly a symbol of her love lost, and a last hope that they would soon be reunited in the next life. Alas, her hopes did not come true, neither in the location of the earrings before death nor in the reuniting of the two lovers...yet.

Envy leaned into her ear and delivered his customary sting and she turned in response, "Yes, she does look beautiful in them. But isn't it a wonder how we can attach a feeling to an object, and it's even more wondrous to admit that the deep feelings of love that you may have for someone is the real treasure of it all." She began to return to her card game but stopped herself before finishing, "And I'll have you know, just to set the record straight, that all my granddaughter's joy will only feed my own happiness. Now go away, Envy." Then she shooed him away with her hand like a fly. Envy was greatly disappointed because he knew, she didn't just say those words, she felt them. And if something far higher above even these trans-dimensional entities could look inside Envy, to what might be considered the heart and mind of the creature, a creature incapable of love, they might see in a fleeting moment that Envy itself felt deeply the very human emotion that was the make of his being. Envy. And all the ladies at the table turned their empty eye sockets to him and quietly waited for him to leave, making it known that he was no longer welcomed at their table.

Wrath is positively fuming throughout the morning. He works as the fireman of the train, shoveling coal into the boiler to keep the steam coming. The steward gave him this additional duty because Wrath would spend his entire evening in the corner of a car waiting. He never engaged with the guests after helping them board the train. He would silently sit but was always uncomfortable, pulling at his collar as though he was just about ready to burst. When he wasn't sitting he was pacing the cars, but this made the guests uneasy. The steward addressed the complaints with Wrath. He said he would make an attempt, and that he did.

It was an eventful dark morning to say the very least as Wrath played a game of chess with a passenger. He had won and won quickly, but when his opponent, Paul, who in life was one of the angriest people Wrath had the pleasure of knowing, congratulated him and applauded his skill, he could contain himself no longer. Chess pieces flew across the car and the table was upended. Then in the blink of an eye there stood the steward in the doorway, stoic in his grey jacket and piercing stare. He pointed at Wrath and beckoned him to come with him without a word. Wrath pushed passed him in the doorway and he was not seen again that morning, and hardly seen after boarding every morning after.

Wrath has little patience and it's hard for him, pretending to play nice. The steward knows it's better to leave him be, shoveling the coal and tending to the fires. Here on the purgatory train the other sins do not seem to have the hold on the souls as they once did, and not one is able to muster enough fuel for Wrath to start any fires of his own. If there was a moment that was just right, he would be there, ready and willing to burn it all to the ground. Those are the moments he dreams of. Wrath is so bitter by the rides end that all the guests have adopted a nickname for him and refer to him secretly as Mr. Killjoy.

Now the spectral passengers are mostly bones and decay by this time of the morning, and their once striking attire hangs off of them in rags. This matter, which they consider minor, brings no discontent to the specters, and as soon as they hear the bow strike the strings of the violins, played in turn by Lust and Pride, they are delighted by the sound of the melody and keep the time of the music with their tapping feet.

Lust is always playing a provocative tango or a sultry waltz, attempting to inspire scandalous behavior; always on the lookout for sideways glances, but to his deep frustration the ghosts are not easily led and aren't enticed by such suggestions. The love seats that align the cars do serve their purpose and inspire love both old and new, but it's not the cheap love that Lust had hoped for. They are seats where stronger bonds grow into everlasting friendships.

But all is not lost as Pride plays The Battle Hymn of the Republic in front of two brothers. Jebidiah, the youngest brother, is dressed in what remains of a Union soldier's uniform. His older brother, Jacob, sits in a decomposing Confederate soldier's uniform. Both began riding this train after meeting their fates on the same battlefield by the blade of each other's bayonet. Pride played almost through the whole song but could not contain his irritation when the brothers started enthusiastically singing the song together. When they embraced near the end Pride could take it no more and threw the violin to the ground and stepped on it. He turned and marched from the car outraged and defeated. No one knew that all along Wrath glared from behind a curtain and watched the scene. When the brothers began to sing together and embrace, Wrath rolled his eyes in disgust and went back to the boiler room.

The car was quiet and the phantoms shifted a little uncomfortably for the first time all morning. Then the steward came in. He extended his hand toward Lust who reluctantly handed him his violin, and the steward began to merrily play one song that did not end until the dancing did. Until he witnessed, like time and time again, the last apparition fall down to dust and bones on the car floor. Then he called the crewmen in.

Right before sunrise and moments before they arrive back to their destination in The Proper, all Seven Sins grab their brooms and sweep the piles of bones and dust to the exits. The steward inspects the train, checking the beds, under the tables, and in the quieter corners of the cars to be certain that all of the passengers will be departing. When they come to a stop the steward instructs the crewmen to sweep the dust and bones out into the lot by the dilapidated depot. Then the train pulls away, blowing its whistle only minutes before sunrise. What is left in the lot for several strange moments is a temporary boneyard: jaw bones, piles of dust, flecks of clothing, femurs, and ribs, existing only until the first sun rays reach it. Then all that remains sinks back into the earth and the specters return to the world of the dormant spirits…. That is just until midnight the next evening of course.

If you're out any time soon around midnight in The Proper and you hear the toll of the church bells you may also hear the whistle of a ghostly pale engine coming down the tracks. Listen closely for the dragon-like sigh when it comes to a stop in front of its passengers. If you are incredibly lucky you may witness the steam roll up into the sky from viperous nostrils and see the moonlight reflected in the diamond skulls resting in the eye sockets of the snake head above the engine. You may also happen to see an assembly of silver shadows in the lot. If you do make sure to be kind and say hello, they are after all just waiting for their train. Of course these apparitions are very hard to see as the environmental conditions must be optimal for it: just the right temperature, just the right amount of moonlight, and at just the right time. Not all will be able to see it in their lifetime, but some will certainly see it afterward.

POETRY

(Song Lyrics)

A dark trail, a lantern
Don't know where I'm going even if I wanted to
The North Star shines in the sky tonight
I reached into my pocket to retrieve a little map I drew
But...

My compass rose is broken, muddled with all words unspoken
Long ago the rose was snipped and left was thorns
But I'll move by intuition till my hopes come to fruition
To the distance river where my soul was born

I will stare at my reflection till my heart finds new direction
And I'll cast away confusion and self doubt
Oh, the silence is my pleasure, but I will sing in any measure
And my heart will reap the harvest in the drought

Divinity, the quiet night, the lightning sparks the fire light
Those distant winds will push me forward, to signs in foreign
languages
My sweater is so very warm and I have never been the norm
But there's a place for me within the arms of you

Poetry, I said, are just words on paper lying dead
Till someone says those written words out loud
Like some lovely spell, if those words are spoken well
It's bound to make the wicked walls fall down

THE LOVE STORY OF OUR DEAREST CLETUS AND ELVIRA

Hark! Hark! All you halfwits, all you daft plebs and crones!
Clean out your ears and set down your phones!
There's a story of love, Cupid's bow found two hearts
And I mean love, Love's true love, and not Lust's rusty darts!

Its symbol is cast upon a steely train trestle
'Cause such love cannot be contained within two mortal vessels!
It must be expressed! It must be displayed!
And we know that symbols on trestles, the bright sun cannot fade!
To win Love's truest love means you are certainly winning
And the longer love lives the more its path begins spinning

I can't tell the whole story, no indeed, I cannot!
But I will tell you, these two lovers, they never were caught!
They painted their heart with prosecutable swagger.
One was the lookout and one was the tagger.

It's clear, by this illicit symbol, that love might inspire sinning,
But I'll tell you what I know, so let's start at Love's beginning.

(que the interrogation light)

In a Piggly Wiggly on a hill, in the blue starless skies of day
Between two facing feet of fate, a broken jar of pickles lay.
They looked at such a dreadful mess, a blocked path between these
fated two.
Shards of glass lay underfoot and pickle juice on toes like
morning's dew.
But when their lovely eyes did meet, they truly held and locked.
Then Cupid's arrow hit with the precise strike of a hawk.
Cletus took off his jacket, with sincere and chivalrous class,
Laid it over all the pickles, all the juice and all the glass.
Elvira stepped across the puddle when he held out his sweaty hand.
And this is where the love story of Cletus and Elvira began.

Several months did pass in Destiny's rapturous bliss.
The day did come when two love birds wed, love sealed with True
Love's kiss.
In the parking lot of the Piggly Wiggly, Aphrodite blushed at
Passion's perfect vow.
And they swore their love to one another under the lit grin of a
sow.

Then after dark they ran like two spry ninjas in the night,
With cans of paint to spray a heart, then their initials they did
write.
Under painted heart and moon, in the throes of all that Cupid
brings
Those two beheld the spell of love, and two hearts beat like angel's
wings

(kill the interrogation light)

Now, their symbol of love adorns that steely, stout train trestle,
Near the wild running waters, where the amorous perch do wrestle.
A symbol to remind me that love is not tame!
It starts with a spark then turns to a flame!

Can I forgive such an illicit proclamation? Yea! I truly can.
'Cause love can bring you to your knees, and that's true of any
man.
So let us give them our blessings! Most kindly raise your glass!
And pray that they keep their truest love as the trials of life do
pass!

So when you take a turn about the park by the steely, stout train
trestle,
And you see the heart near flowing water, where the amorous
perch do wrestle,
Send your love to Cletus and Elvira, say a prayer for love and
passion!
Long live the shot of Cupid's bow! And may painted hearts never
go out of fashion!

THE ACTORS THEATER

Welcome to the theater!
Have a seat! Come on in!
You don't even know half the time an act is going to begin!
Mind the fools, and the whores, and all their wild rumpus!
However…
Most theater IS inspired by a poor moral compass.
Now, if you are afflicted, like me, with a blazing, crazed temper
Don't let it be food for a calculating contender.
If you are quick to true anger they will attempt to rule it.
They're not stupid, they're smart, so we must work our way
through it.
Opportunist they are. Oh! A Victim! They're it! …….
And you're on their radar, 'cause they thrive in the shit.
Once they've worked up our frenzy, and drawn a crowd near,
They throw themselves on your sword for the sake of the theater.
"Woe! Woe! Woe is me!" They say.
"What a terrible person! What a terrible day!
Look at mine eyes. Wild tears, how they fall!
I'm a tiny little mouse under a great tiger's paw!"
(sigh)
Now,
now,
now
We must admit our own fault with our vicious, biting anger.
Ass out on a stage in a room full of strangers.
And the acting so good one can hardly compare,

You can hardly believe the Academy's not there!
The hooting, the snapping, from the theater savants
And all will forget... that anger was a valid response.
A response to what? The people hardly do care,
They see a terrified mouse, and a rabid, wild bear!

But creatures we are, and if we think then we'll find
(THE TRUTH!)
It's better to laugh than to spoil the good wine.

Now, we must also admit we're not little mouse creatures.
We don't construct scenes to be spotlighted features.
So, I asked, and you asked, and we asked for a way
To keep peace in our hearts when one tries to strip it away.
And because we asked, and we looked, we were given a gift.
It has not been easy, it required a great shift.
Some may think we're crazy, certifiably insane!
But there are many whose presence
we
will
no
longer
entertain,
Because…
When you grow your sound heart, and you polish your grit
You'll no longer waste time on that same kind of shit.

Now we will sleep soundly in our peaceful, little houses
Because we are the tigers and not the measly little mouses.

ODE TO SPRING

Sugary Spring with your buttercup buttons
Place your breezy arms around me in an enchanting embrace
To your cherished virtue I am a glutton and there's no greater
beauty than your blooming face
Oh, gentle sister of Summer with such revitalizing grace
Never as harsh as your Winter brother whose barren landscape you
replace

The bullfrog's siren calls to me amongst the lily pads in the pool
The Juncos in the Juniper, The spider spins its spool
The lantern of the fireflies, The dew of morning's drool
Your day becomes my carriage, your night becomes my fuel

Lady bug jeweled leaves, the lizard's swift agility
Floret blankets under feathered clouds, green mountains of nobility
Delightful dancing of the bees, the daisy's refined tranquility
The budding beauty of the rose holds my heart implicitly

Beloved Spring in your gentle arms I'll lay whether mountain top
or deep green meadow
In your grace I long to stay, down the flowered forest path
overgrown and narrow
Amongst the honeysuckle's bloom is where I'll spend my day, the
cricket's song as piercing as an arrow
And then my heart will become the lovely rose of May and my
soul the sparrow

I KNOW NO BRAVER MAN

(A poem on Veteran's Day)

I know no braver man than the man who raised me, and his brother.

Nor the man who raised them and the man who raised my Mother.

Each one a Veteran, some are here and some are gone.

They were taught to be soldiers, to fight, then carry on,

From the top of metal helmets down to worn and tired boots,

With their rifles in their hands, and on their backs they wore parachutes.

They never cared for glory or no bloody recognition.

But they cared for one another and a good supply of ammunition.

Some returned with shrapnel, some with memories sealed in stone.

Some with scars across their bodies, some with scars within their bones.

But each one a great example of what one man can do,

A battle-weary body but their spirits pulling through.

And they returned to love, and love indeed they did.

And they held me in their arms when I was just a little kid.

I did not know their glory because they would call it none.

I did not know their sacrifice because my life had just begun.

But now I do, Lord, now I do! I've been blessed to know the lot!

I've been blessed to know the men the wicked wars had never got!

Dear God bless the soldier, your name on lips they hold.

They did not forget the prayers they said before they fell into the folds.

Down in the foxhole, weeks of monsoon rain,

Ascending up 'round, endless mountain boulder,

All the things they had to do when they were branded as a soldier.

I'll hold it high above my head like a treasure to be saved.

And I will celebrate this day because their valor

Shall

Not

Fade.

TENT

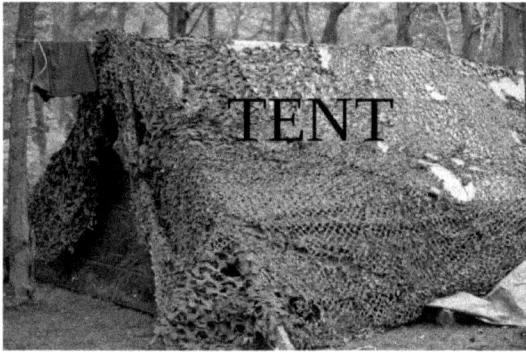

We arrived at the camping grounds. The bed of a truck filled with 2x4s, tarps, stakes, and ropes. This was not a store bought contraption but homemade. This was TENT. Not A tent. Not THE tent. Just TENT. It was assembled in a clearing of the forest. Setup was an hour or more. (Heave! Ho! Heave! Ho!) We raised our flag. We were established. And then we stood in the turret and peered down at the other campers in their flimsy polyester housing, with their fancy zippers and optional skylights, and shouted, "I spit on your tent!" (over dramatization, we didn't really have a turret) Needless to say, we didn't appear to be "run of the mill" campers but more like gypsy carpenters with a mountain man as a foreman.

My father had spent many a day constructing this masterpiece and to my mother's dismay it stood assembled in the front yard of their home for weeks. During that time there were days you could peek inside and see my father asleep on an old army cot. Maybe this is the real reason why my mother disliked it, since she doesn't believe in naps. She believes naps are for the weak. It's time wasted! Why sleep when you could be painting an ocean scene on the walls, laying down tile, or rearranging furniture. My mother is like a kinetic watch. No winding with a self-charging battery. She can function fully on 4 hours of sleep with no mental lag. TENT caused my Mother stress. I am certain on more than one occasion my Mother threw her hands up in frustration. TENT was casting way too much shade on her perennials. TENT had become the sneaky nap room and her honey-do-list was accumulating dust. And finally TENT wasn't built for beauty but was constructed to withstand the elements. Eventually my mother got tired of seeing it dominate her front yard with its powerful presence. It appeared that my mother was stronger than the elements because eventually TENT came down.

But the day did come when we assembled TENT in a clearing in the woods. There were other campers in the area, some you could see in the distance through the trees with their Pop Up tents that might not withstand strong gusts of 5 mph winds or a torrential slight drizzle. By the look of it, (the downward glances, the absence of waves) our neighboring campers didn't know if we were traveling gypsies, a hoard of geniuses, or a pack of lunatics, and the fear that inspired them to keep their distance suited us just fine. We are a fine people that enjoy each other's company. We talk about everything from war to poetry. Swapping recipes and drinking coffee. We don't like to argue but enjoy debate and aren't intimidated by differences of opinions. (We know we're right anyway.)

There were two rooms, an outer room much like a covered porch and the inner room with a tarp laid over the forest floor, and on that an inflated air mattress. The outer room held two army cots. Fallen tree branches were collected as well as twigs and dry grass for kindling. The stocked cooler was placed nearby and the chairs set around the fire. We sat in the chairs and the children frolicked about and we all enjoyed the new scenery and serenity of the tall trees around us. My two daughters as well as myself were in attendance. This was many years ago so they were quite younger.

A good while after nightfall when our bellies were full of s'mores and hot dogs, after we listened to the fire crackling and watched sparks of embers rise up with the smoke, my children and

I called it a day. We settled down, snug as a bug in the bedding on the air mattress of TENT's inner room. The fire was going still, and others in attendance were enjoying the night, but we were tired and the three of us closed our eyes for sleep.

I heard a noise. It was an animal. Near the position of my head was a tarp wall but behind that was the tree line. I opened my eyes briefly, still mostly asleep, and then closed them just as quickly. I was in the woods. These are not unusual sounds. Then again I heard the noise. It wasn't just movement, but a soft repetitive barking sound near my head. Now I was awake. I was awake as though I had never slept. It was totally dark. I had no idea what time it was. I reached for a battery powered lantern, hit the switch, and I swung it toward my children. Sophia, my oldest daughter, was wide eyed and terrified. "Did you hear that?" She whispered. I nodded. I looked through the opening of the tarp of the inner room, out to the covered entryway. I could see my father asleep on a cot fully clothed. His boots were still on. No covers. No pillow. That kind of sleep he'd fallen into thousands of times before. The luxuries are for losers sleep. The army sleep. And I will never forget this next moment, because it says a lot about the man my father is. I said in my normal tone of voice, "Dad, there is something outside of the tent."

It was like he was never asleep at all. He needed no clarification of what I said due to any sort of grogginess. I did not have to repeat myself or try to wake him. It was as though he was alert at all times. Immediately, he stood and without hesitation or light, he left the tent to find the source of the noise. Unafraid, out into the darkness of the woods.

My father has always said the night is your friend. The only thing that can hurt you is another man. Animals will try to avoid you. He has told us many times about different night events that happened either in war or throughout his army career. My father can function just fine in the night. The darkness does not scare him and I know there have been times in his life when nightfall couldn't come soon enough. It kept him safe, more concealed. The night lays its darkness and shadows down on all things, a camouflage and our eyes are not designed to see well in the dark. I remember him telling me once that if you are quiet and lay down in the woods a man could walk right by you and never know you are there. This gives me the chills and not because my father would be anyone to be afraid of in the dark, my father would cook you a meal and give you the shirt off his back, but it gives me the chills because my father probably has experienced this in his life; where someone who meant to do him harm was close, and to survive he had to lay silently still in the cover of the night.

When he returned to the cot he said all was well. It was just an animal and when he laid down to sleep we all knew that it was true. All was well. We slept soundly till morning.

MY GRANDFATHER WAS
THE GREAT VAMPIRE SLAYER

(Song Lyrics)

My Grandfather was The Great Vampire Slayer
He taught me all that he knows
His crosses, blessed water, his stakes, and his prayer
So, I'll be the next one I suppose

As a baby he held me so tightly
He rocked me to sleep with a verse
"My girl, one day with the power of prayer
You'll fight the world's deadliest curse"

"You are the light of the world
A town on a hill can't be hidden" (Matthew 5: 14)
Your yoke won't be easy, your burden not light (Matthew 11: 30
reversed)
But down this pure path you'll be driven

At nightfall my Grandfather would say to me
When the sunlight would say its goodbye
Psalm 23, because he could see
The Vampire Slayer inside

One hundred battles I fought by his side
Since he gave me the tools of the trade
He taught me my courage, he taught me my pride
What a true and fierce fighter he's made

I won't forget the night my Grandfather died
We set out to kill and to conquer
I stayed by his side, oh, how I cried
Then I cut off the head of that monster

Dear Grandfather you'll always be remembered
Your trials are all over, your sins are forgiven
Since the Lord is my Shepherd I'll walk down this path
I'll cherish this road I've been given

My Grandfather was The Great Vampire Slayer
He taught me all that he knows
His crosses, blessed water, his stakes, and his prayer
I'll be the next Vampire Slayer
I am the next Vampire Slayer
The last of the Vampire Slayers
I suppose

ABOUT THE AUTHOR

A.K. Williams is an author who enjoys playing guitar at her kitchen table. She writes poetry and song lyrics in her spare time. She is a wife of 21 years and a mother of two young ladies. She loves a good ghost story, adores folklore, and resides in the state of Kentucky.